Balsamic Vinegar Cookbook

Exploring the Rich Flavors and Versatility of Balsamic Vinegar in 20 Delicious Recipes

BALSAMIC VINEGAR COOKBOOK

First edition. October 24, 2023.

ISBN: 979-8223785347

Written by Sammy Andrews.

Sammy Andrews

Introduction to Balsamic Vinegar

Balsamic Vinegar Basics

Balsamic Vinegar in Salad Dressings

Appetizers with a Tangy Twist

Balsamic-Glazed Meats

Seafood Delights with Balsamic Flare

Vegetarian and Vegan Balsamic Creations

- Roasted balsamic vegetables
- Balsamic-glazed tofu
- Stuffed portobello mushrooms with balsamic drizzle

Balsamic in Soups and Stews

- Tomato basil soup with balsamic swirl
- Balsamic-infused vegetable stew
- Balsamic chicken noodle soup

Balsamic Pasta Perfection

- Balsamic pasta primavera
- Creamy balsamic fettuccine
- Balsamic and sun-dried tomato spaghetti

Balsamic Rice and Grains

- Balsamic risotto with mushrooms
- Balsamic-infused quinoa salad
- Wild rice with balsamic glaze

Balsamic in Sides and Dips

- Balsamic roasted potatoes
- Balsamic Brussels sprouts
- Balsamic caramelized onions and dip

Balsamic Desserts

- Balsamic berry compote
- Balsamic chocolate truffles
- Balsamic vanilla ice cream

- Tasting notes and pairings

Balsamic Vinegar as a Gift

- Packaging and presentation
- Creating balsamic gift sets
- Homemade balsamic gift ideas

Conclusion and Beyond

- Recap of balsamic adventures
- Exploring further balsamic possibilities
- Resources and references

Chapter 1: Introduction to Balsamic Vinegar

Unveiling the Rich History and Versatility of Balsamic Vinegar

Balsamic vinegar, with its complex flavors and deep, dark hues, has long been a beloved condiment in the culinary world. It's more than just a salad dressing; it's a culinary treasure with a history as rich as its taste. In this chapter, we'll embark on a journey to discover the origins of balsamic vinegar, explore the various types available, and learn how to choose the best balsamic vinegar for your culinary creations.

The Rich History of Balsamic Vinegar

Balsamic vinegar's history dates back to ancient times. It has its roots in Italy, specifically in the regions of Modena and Reggio Emilia. The first mentions of balsamic vinegar can be traced as far back as the 11th century, where it was used both for culinary purposes and for its purported medicinal benefits.

The word "balsamic" itself is derived from the Latin word "balsamum," which means "restorative." This is a testament to the historical belief in the vinegar's health benefits.

The Production Process

Balsamic vinegar is not your ordinary vinegar. It's a product of careful craftsmanship and patience. Traditionally, it's made from the juice (or must) of freshly crushed grapes. Here's an overview of the production process:

Grape Selection: The grapes used are typically Trebbiano and Lambrusco varieties. These grapes are harvested at their ripest, ensuring the best flavor.

Cooking the Must: The grape must is simmered over an open flame, reducing it to a concentrated syrup. This process can take hours and is crucial to the vinegar's flavor profile.

Aging in Wooden Barrels: The concentrated must is transferred to a series of wooden barrels, often made of different types of wood like oak, chestnut, cherry, and juniper. The aging process in these barrels can range from several years to several decades, imparting distinct flavors and complexity to the vinegar.

Blending and Bottling: After aging, the vinegar is carefully blended to achieve the desired flavor profile. It's then bottled and labeled according to its age and quality.

Types of Balsamic Vinegar

Not all balsamic vinegar is created equal. There are several types of balsamic vinegar, each with its own characteristics and uses:

Traditional Balsamic Vinegar (Aceto Balsamico Tradizionale): This is the highest quality balsamic vinegar and is aged for a minimum of 12 years, often much longer. It has a thick, syrupy consistency and a complex, sweet-tart flavor. Use it sparingly as a drizzle over desserts, cheeses, or grilled meats.

Balsamic Vinegar of Modena (Aceto Balsamico di Modena): This is the most common type found in supermarkets. It's still high quality but is aged for a shorter period, usually a minimum of two months. It has a well-balanced sweet and tangy flavor and is versatile for various culinary applications.

Aged Balsamic Vinegar: Some producers offer balsamic vinegar aged for longer periods, such as 5, 10, or 25 years. These are often prized for their complexity and depth of flavor.

Flavored Balsamic Vinegar: Infused or flavored balsamic vinegars are becoming increasingly popular. They come in a variety of flavors, including fruit-infused, herb-infused, and even chocolate-infused balsamic vinegars. These are excellent for adding unique flavors to your dishes.

Choosing the Best Balsamic Vinegar

When selecting balsamic vinegar for your recipes, consider the following:

Label Information: Look for indications of quality and origin on the label. Traditional balsamic vinegar should be labeled as such, while Modena balsamic vinegar should specify the aging period.

Ingredients: Check the ingredient list. High-quality balsamic vinegar should contain only grape must and wine vinegar, with no additives or artificial flavors.

Taste and Aroma: A good balsamic vinegar should have a balanced sweet and tangy taste with a pleasant aroma. You can often sample the vinegar before purchasing, so take advantage of this if possible.

Packaging: Balsamic vinegar is sensitive to light and air. Choose vinegar that comes in dark glass bottles to protect it from degradation.

As we delve further into this cookbook, you'll discover how balsamic vinegar can elevate your culinary creations, from salad dressings to desserts and everything in between. So, let's embark on this flavorful journey and unlock the incredible potential of balsamic vinegar in your kitchen.

Chapter 2: Balsamic Vinegar Basics

Unveiling the Secrets Behind Balsamic Vinegar Production and More

Balsamic vinegar is a true artisanal product, and understanding its basics is essential to make the most of its unique flavors and applications. In this chapter, we'll delve into the production process of balsamic vinegar, explore the significance of aging for its quality, and discuss the proper storage and handling techniques to preserve its integrity.

Understanding the Production Process

Balsamic vinegar is not just a simple condiment; it's a product of intricate craftsmanship that dates back centuries. To truly appreciate it, let's take a closer look at the steps involved in its production:

1. Grape Selection

The journey of balsamic vinegar begins with the careful selection of grapes. The two primary grape varieties used are Trebbiano and Lambrusco. These grapes are chosen for their ideal balance of sweetness and acidity.

2. Cooking the Must

The grape must, which is freshly crushed grape juice, is simmered in open pots over a direct flame. This slow-cooking process can last for hours and is crucial for concentrating the flavors and sugars.

3. Aging in Wooden Barrels

One of the most distinctive aspects of balsamic vinegar production is its aging in wooden barrels. These barrels are often made from various types of wood, including oak, chestnut, cherry, and juniper. The aging process takes place over several years, sometimes even decades. During this time, the vinegar undergoes a transformation, absorbing the complex flavors and aromas from the wood.

Size Matters: The size of the barrels also plays a role in the vinegar's development. Smaller barrels allow for greater interaction with the wood, resulting in a more pronounced wood influence.

Evaporation and Concentration: As the vinegar ages, it slowly evaporates through the wood's pores. This evaporation concentrates the vinegar and contributes to its thick, syrupy texture.

Blending and Bottling

After the aging process, balsamic vinegar is carefully blended to achieve the desired flavor profile. It's essential to maintain consistency, especially for those vinegars labeled with specific aging categories. Once the vinegar is perfected, it's bottled and labeled according to its age and quality.

Aging and Quality

The age of balsamic vinegar significantly influences its quality and flavor profile. Here's a breakdown of the aging categories you might encounter:

Young Balsamic Vinegar: Aged for a minimum of two months, young balsamic vinegar is characterized by a well-balanced sweet and tangy flavor. It's versatile and suitable for various culinary applications.

Aged Balsamic Vinegar: With aging periods ranging from 5 years to 25 years or more, aged balsamic vinegars develop a more complex flavor profile. They become thicker, richer, and often exhibit notes of wood, fruit, and spices.

Traditional Balsamic Vinegar (Aceto Balsamico Tradizionale): The pinnacle of balsamic vinegar quality, traditional balsamic vinegar is aged for a minimum of 12 years, sometimes up to 25 years or longer. It has a syrupy consistency and boasts an incredibly complex and nuanced flavor profile.

Proper Storage and Handling

To ensure the longevity and quality of your balsamic vinegar, follow these essential storage and handling tips:

Store in a Cool, Dark Place: Balsamic vinegar is sensitive to light and temperature fluctuations. Keep it in a cool, dark cupboard away from direct sunlight and heat sources.

Seal Tightly: Always seal the bottle tightly after each use to prevent air from entering, which can cause oxidation.

Avoid Refrigeration: While it's essential to keep balsamic vinegar cool, refrigeration can cause it to thicken and become syrupy. It's best stored at room temperature.

Check for Sediment: Over time, sediment may form at the bottom of the bottle. This is natural and harmless. Simply shake the bottle gently before use to mix it back in.

Understanding the production process, aging, and proper storage and handling of balsamic vinegar sets the foundation for your culinary adventures with this remarkable condiment. In the chapters that follow, we'll explore its diverse applications, from salad dressings to desserts, and uncover the full spectrum of flavors it can bring to your dishes.

Chapter 3: Balsamic Vinegar in Salad Dressings

Elevate Your Greens with the Magic of Balsamic Vinegar

Salads are a canvas for flavor, and balsamic vinegar is the brush that paints a masterpiece. In this chapter, we'll explore the art of crafting sensational salad dressings using balsamic vinegar. Whether you prefer the classic balsamic vinaigrette, crave the sweetness of fruit-infused dressings, or indulge in the creaminess of balsamic creams, we've got your salad game covered.

Classic Balsamic Vinaigrette

The classic balsamic vinaigrette is a timeless favorite, celebrated for its harmonious blend of tangy and sweet flavors. It's incredibly versatile and pairs well with a wide range of salads, from simple garden greens to more complex creations. Here's a basic recipe to get you started:

Ingredients:

- 3 tablespoons extra-virgin olive oil
- 1 tablespoon balsamic vinegar
- 1 teaspoon Dijon mustard
- 1 clove garlic, minced (optional)
- Salt and freshly ground black pepper to taste

Instructions:

Whisk Together: In a small bowl, whisk together the balsamic vinegar, Dijon mustard, minced garlic (if using), salt, and pepper until well combined.

Drizzle in the Olive Oil: While whisking continuously, slowly drizzle in the extra-virgin olive oil. This gradual incorporation emulsifies the dressing, creating a creamy texture.

Taste and Adjust: Taste the dressing and adjust the seasoning if needed. You can add more balsamic vinegar for tanginess or olive oil to mellow the flavor.

Serve: Drizzle the vinaigrette over your favorite salad just before serving, and toss gently to coat the greens evenly.

Fruit-Infused Dressings

Fruit-infused balsamic dressings offer a delightful twist to your salads, introducing sweet and fruity notes that complement the freshness of your greens. Here are a couple of fruit-infused dressing ideas:

Balsamic Strawberry Dressing
Ingredients:

- 1/2 cup fresh strawberries, hulled and halved
- 3 tablespoons balsamic vinegar
- 2 tablespoons extra-virgin olive oil
- 1 teaspoon honey (optional)
- Salt and freshly ground black pepper to taste

Instructions:

Blend: In a blender or food processor, combine the strawberries, balsamic vinegar, olive oil, and honey (if using). Blend until smooth.

Season: Season the dressing with a pinch of salt and freshly ground black pepper to taste.

Serve: Drizzle this luscious strawberry-balsamic dressing over a mixed greens salad, and garnish with additional strawberry slices if desired.

Balsamic Fig Dressing
Ingredients:

- 4-5 dried figs, rehydrated in hot water and chopped
- 3 tablespoons balsamic vinegar
- 2 tablespoons extra-virgin olive oil
- 1 teaspoon honey (optional)
- Salt and freshly ground black pepper to taste

Instructions:

Prepare the Figs: Rehydrate the dried figs by placing them in a bowl of hot water for about 15 minutes. Drain and chop the figs.

Blend: In a blender or food processor, combine the chopped figs, balsamic vinegar, olive oil, and honey (if using). Blend until the dressing is smooth.

Season: Add a pinch of salt and freshly ground black pepper to taste.

Serve: This fig-balsamic dressing pairs beautifully with arugula, goat cheese, and candied pecans for a gourmet salad experience.

Creamy Balsamic Dressings

If you're looking for a luxurious and velvety dressing, creamy balsamic options are the way to go. Creamy balsamic dressings are a delightful departure from the traditional vinaigrettes, offering a rich and indulgent texture. Here's a simple recipe:

Creamy Balsamic Caesar Dressing
Ingredients:

- 1/4 cup mayonnaise
- 2 tablespoons balsamic vinegar
- 1 clove garlic, minced
- 1 teaspoon Dijon mustard
- 1/4 cup grated Parmesan cheese
- Salt and freshly ground black pepper to taste

Instructions:

Whisk Together: In a bowl, whisk together the mayonnaise, balsamic vinegar, minced garlic, Dijon mustard, and grated Parmesan cheese until smooth.

Season: Add salt and freshly ground black pepper to taste.

Serve: This creamy balsamic Caesar dressing is perfect for romaine lettuce salads, topped with croutons and additional Parmesan cheese.

These balsamic vinegar-infused dressings will elevate your salad experience to a whole new level. Feel free to experiment with different fruits, herbs, and other ingredients to create your unique dressings and take your salads from ordinary to extraordinary.

Chapter 4: Appetizers with a Tangy Twist

Elevate Your Appetizer Game with Balsamic Vinegar

Balsamic vinegar adds a tantalizing tangy twist to your appetizers, transforming ordinary bites into extraordinary starters. In this chapter, we'll explore three delightful appetizer recipes that showcase the versatility and rich flavors of balsamic vinegar.

Balsamic Glazed Bruschetta

Balsamic glazed bruschetta is a crowd-pleaser that combines the richness of balsamic vinegar with the freshness of ripe tomatoes and fragrant basil. This classic Italian appetizer is the perfect way to whet your guests' appetites.

Ingredients:

- 1 baguette, cut into 1/2-inch slices
- 3 ripe tomatoes, diced
- 1/4 cup fresh basil leaves, chopped
- 2 cloves garlic, minced
- 1/4 cup extra-virgin olive oil
- 2 tablespoons balsamic vinegar
- Salt and freshly ground black pepper to taste

Instructions:

Toast the Baguette Slices: Preheat your oven's broiler. Arrange the baguette slices on a baking sheet and place them under the broiler for 1-2 minutes per side until they are lightly toasted. Keep an eye on them to prevent burning.

Prepare the Tomato Mixture: In a bowl, combine the diced tomatoes, chopped basil, minced garlic, extra-virgin olive oil, and balsamic vinegar. Season with salt and freshly ground black pepper to taste. Toss the mixture gently to combine all the flavors.

Assemble the Bruschetta: Once the baguette slices are toasted, remove them from the oven. Spoon the tomato mixture generously over each slice.

Serve: Arrange the balsamic glazed bruschetta on a platter and serve immediately. Enjoy the burst of flavors in every bite!

Caprese Skewers with Balsamic Reduction

Caprese skewers with balsamic reduction are a delightful and elegant appetizer that combines the classic flavors of Caprese salad with the intensity of balsamic reduction. These bite-sized wonders are perfect for parties and gatherings.

Ingredients:

- Cherry tomatoes
- Fresh mozzarella balls (small size)
- Fresh basil leaves
- Balsamic reduction (store-bought or homemade)

Instructions:

Assemble the Skewers: Thread one cherry tomato, one mozzarella ball, and one fresh basil leaf onto small skewers or toothpicks. Repeat until you have enough skewers for your guests.

Drizzle with Balsamic Reduction: Arrange the skewers on a serving platter, and just before serving, drizzle them generously with balsamic reduction. The sweet and tangy reduction will elevate the flavors of the Caprese skewers.

Serve: These Caprese skewers are ready to impress. Your guests will love the burst of flavor in each bite, highlighted by the balsamic reduction.

Balsamic-Marinated Olives

Balsamic-marinated olives are a savory and tangy appetizer that pairs perfectly with a glass of wine or aperitif. These olives are marinated in a flavorful blend of balsamic vinegar, herbs, and spices.

Ingredients:

- 1 cup assorted olives (green, Kalamata, etc.), pitted
- 2 tablespoons balsamic vinegar

- 1 clove garlic, minced
- 1 teaspoon dried oregano
- 1/2 teaspoon red pepper flakes (adjust to taste)
- Zest of 1 lemon
- 2 tablespoons extra-virgin olive oil
- Fresh parsley for garnish (optional)

Instructions:

Prepare the Marinade: In a bowl, whisk together the balsamic vinegar, minced garlic, dried oregano, red pepper flakes, and lemon zest. Slowly drizzle in the extra-virgin olive oil while whisking to emulsify the marinade.

Marinate the Olives: Place the pitted olives in a container or a bowl and pour the balsamic marinade over them. Toss the olives to coat them evenly with the marinade.

Chill and Serve: Cover the container and refrigerate the olives for at least 2 hours, allowing them to marinate and soak up the flavors. Before serving, bring the olives to room temperature and garnish with fresh parsley if desired.

These appetizers with a tangy twist will set the stage for an unforgettable dining experience. Whether you're hosting a gathering or simply indulging in some flavorful bites, these recipes showcase the magic of balsamic vinegar in your culinary creations.

Chapter 5: Balsamic-Glazed Meats

Elevate Your Meat Dishes with Balsamic Vinegar

Balsamic vinegar brings depth and complexity to meat dishes, creating a delightful contrast between the rich flavors of the meat and the sweet tanginess of the vinegar. In this chapter, we'll explore two tantalizing recipes that showcase the art of balsamic-glazed meats.

Balsamic Glazed Chicken Breasts

Balsamic glazed chicken breasts are a perfect harmony of flavors, combining tender, juicy chicken with the rich sweetness of balsamic vinegar. This dish is quick to prepare and perfect for a weeknight dinner or a special occasion.

Ingredients:

- 4 boneless, skinless chicken breasts
- 1/2 cup balsamic vinegar
- 1/4 cup honey
- 2 cloves garlic, minced
- 1 teaspoon dried rosemary
- Salt and freshly ground black pepper to taste
- Fresh rosemary sprigs for garnish (optional)

Instructions:

Prepare the Glaze: In a small saucepan, combine the balsamic vinegar, honey, minced garlic, dried rosemary, salt, and freshly ground black pepper. Bring the mixture to a simmer over medium heat. Reduce the heat and let it simmer for about 10-15 minutes, or until the glaze thickens and reduces by half. Remove it from heat and set aside.

Cook the Chicken: Season the chicken breasts with a pinch of salt and freshly ground black pepper. Heat a grill or grill pan over medium-high heat. Grill the chicken for about 5-7 minutes per side, or until the internal temperature reaches 165°F (74°C) and the chicken is cooked through.

Glaze the Chicken: Brush the balsamic glaze generously over the grilled chicken during the last few minutes of cooking. Allow the glaze to caramelize and create a flavorful coating on the chicken.

Serve: Transfer the balsamic glazed chicken breasts to a serving platter, garnish with fresh rosemary sprigs if desired, and drizzle any remaining glaze over the top. Serve hot and enjoy the burst of flavors!

Grilled Balsamic Steak

Grilled balsamic steak is a carnivore's delight, offering the perfect balance of savory meat and sweet, tangy balsamic glaze. This recipe is ideal for those who crave the charred perfection of a grilled steak.

Ingredients:

- 4 boneless ribeye steaks (or your preferred cut)
- 1/2 cup balsamic vinegar
- 2 tablespoons soy sauce
- 2 cloves garlic, minced
- 2 tablespoons brown sugar
- 1 teaspoon dried thyme
- Salt and freshly ground black pepper to taste
- Fresh thyme sprigs for garnish (optional)

Instructions:

Prepare the Marinade: In a bowl, whisk together the balsamic vinegar, soy sauce, minced garlic, brown sugar, dried thyme, salt, and freshly ground black pepper to create the marinade.

Marinate the Steaks: Place the ribeye steaks in a shallow dish and pour the balsamic marinade over them. Ensure that the steaks are well coated. Cover the dish and refrigerate for at least 30 minutes to marinate.

Grill the Steaks: Preheat your grill to high heat. Remove the steaks from the marinade and grill them to your preferred level of doneness, about 3-4 minutes per side for medium-rare, depending on the thickness of the steaks.

Glaze the Steaks: During the last few minutes of grilling, brush the steaks with the balsamic marinade to create a delicious glaze. Allow the glaze to caramelize and impart its sweet and tangy flavor to the meat.

Serve: Transfer the grilled balsamic steaks to a serving platter, garnish with fresh thyme sprigs if desired, and serve hot. Savor the succulent meat and the rich balsamic infusion.

These balsamic-glazed meat dishes will take your taste buds on a savory journey, showcasing the versatility and depth of flavor that balsamic vinegar can bring to your favorite cuts of meat.

Chapter 6: Seafood Delights with Balsamic Flare

Elevate Your Seafood Experience with Balsamic Vinegar

Balsamic vinegar is a natural companion for seafood, enhancing its flavors with a harmonious blend of sweet and tangy notes. In this chapter, we'll dive into the world of seafood delights, featuring three mouthwatering recipes that showcase the exquisite pairing of balsamic vinegar with the ocean's bounty.

Balsamic-Glazed Salmon

Balsamic-glazed salmon is a culinary masterpiece that combines the richness of salmon with the sweet and tangy allure of balsamic vinegar. This dish is not only visually stunning but also a symphony of flavors.

Ingredients:

- 4 salmon fillets
- 1/4 cup balsamic vinegar
- 2 tablespoons honey
- 2 cloves garlic, minced
- 1 tablespoon Dijon mustard
- 1 teaspoon dried thyme
- Salt and freshly ground black pepper to taste
- Fresh thyme sprigs for garnish (optional)

Instructions:

Prepare the Glaze: In a bowl, whisk together the balsamic vinegar, honey, minced garlic, Dijon mustard, dried thyme, salt, and freshly ground black pepper to create the glaze.

Glaze the Salmon: Place the salmon fillets on a baking sheet lined with parchment paper or a greased grill pan. Brush the balsamic glaze generously over the salmon.

Broil or Grill: If using an oven, preheat the broiler. Broil the salmon for about 6-8 minutes, or until it's cooked to your preferred level of doneness and the glaze caramelizes. If using a grill, grill the salmon for approximately 4-6 minutes per side, brushing with additional glaze during cooking.

Serve: Transfer the balsamic-glazed salmon fillets to a serving platter, garnish with fresh thyme sprigs if desired, and serve hot. Enjoy the exquisite blend of flavors!

Shrimp and Scallops in Balsamic Butter Sauce

Shrimp and scallops in balsamic butter sauce is a luxurious dish that brings together the succulence of seafood with the richness of a buttery balsamic reduction. This recipe is perfect for a special occasion or a romantic dinner.

Ingredients:

- 1 pound large shrimp, peeled and deveined
- 1/2 pound sea scallops
- 2 tablespoons olive oil
- 2 cloves garlic, minced
- 1/2 cup chicken or seafood broth
- 1/4 cup balsamic vinegar
- 2 tablespoons unsalted butter
- Salt and freshly ground black pepper to taste
- Chopped fresh parsley for garnish (optional)

Instructions:

Sear the Seafood: Heat the olive oil in a large skillet over medium-high heat. Add the shrimp and scallops to the skillet and cook for about 2-3 minutes per side, or until they turn pink (for shrimp) and develop a golden crust (for scallops). Transfer the cooked seafood to a plate and set aside.

Prepare the Balsamic Butter Sauce: In the same skillet, add the minced garlic and sauté for about 30 seconds until fragrant. Pour in the chicken or seafood broth and balsamic vinegar. Allow the mixture to simmer and reduce by half, approximately 5-7 minutes.

Add the Butter: Reduce the heat to low and whisk in the unsalted butter until it melts and the sauce becomes glossy. Season with salt and freshly ground black pepper to taste.

Combine and Serve: Return the cooked shrimp and scallops to the skillet, tossing them in the balsamic butter sauce until they are well coated and heated through.

Garnish and Serve: Transfer the shrimp and scallops in balsamic butter sauce to a serving platter, garnish with chopped fresh parsley if desired, and serve immediately. Savor the decadent flavors!

Balsamic-Marinated Grilled Prawns

Balsamic-marinated grilled prawns are a delightful appetizer or main course, offering succulent prawns infused with the sweet and tangy essence of balsamic vinegar. These grilled prawns are a true delight for seafood lovers.

Ingredients:

- 1 pound large prawns, peeled and deveined
- 1/4 cup balsamic vinegar
- 2 cloves garlic, minced
- 2 tablespoons extra-virgin olive oil
- 1 tablespoon fresh lemon juice
- 1 teaspoon dried Italian seasoning
- Salt and freshly ground black pepper to taste
- Lemon wedges for garnish (optional)

Instructions:

Prepare the Marinade: In a bowl, whisk together the balsamic vinegar, minced garlic, extra-virgin olive oil, fresh lemon juice, dried Italian seasoning, salt, and freshly ground black pepper to create the marinade.

Marinate the Prawns: Place the peeled and deveined prawns in a shallow dish and pour the balsamic marinade over them. Ensure that the prawns are well coated. Cover the dish and refrigerate for at least 30 minutes to marinate.

Grill the Prawns: Preheat your grill to medium-high heat. Thread the marinated prawns onto skewers. Grill the prawns for about 2-3 minutes per side, or until they turn pink and opaque, with grill marks.

Serve: Transfer the balsamic-marinated grilled prawns to a serving platter, garnish with lemon wedges if desired, and serve hot. Enjoy the delightful burst of flavors!

These seafood delights with a balsamic flare are a testament to the enchanting synergy between balsamic vinegar and the ocean's treasures. Whether you're a seafood aficionado or simply seeking an exquisite culinary experience, these recipes will not disappoint.

Chapter 7: Vegetarian and Vegan Balsamic Creations

Elevate Your Plant-Based Dishes with the Magic of Balsamic Vinegar

Balsamic vinegar is a versatile ingredient that adds depth and complexity to vegetarian and vegan dishes, creating delightful flavors that will satisfy your taste buds. In this chapter, we'll explore three delectable recipes that showcase the creativity of vegetarian and vegan cooking with balsamic vinegar.

Roasted Balsamic Vegetables

Roasted balsamic vegetables are a symphony of flavors, where the natural sweetness of vegetables meets the tangy richness of balsamic vinegar. This dish is simple to prepare and makes a perfect side or main course for vegetarians and vegans alike.

Ingredients:

- Assorted vegetables (e.g., bell peppers, zucchini, cherry tomatoes, red onions, mushrooms)
- 1/4 cup balsamic vinegar
- 2 tablespoons extra-virgin olive oil
- 2 cloves garlic, minced
- 1 teaspoon dried Italian seasoning
- Salt and freshly ground black pepper to taste
- Fresh basil leaves for garnish (optional)

Instructions:

Prepare the Marinade: In a bowl, whisk together the balsamic vinegar, extra-virgin olive oil, minced garlic, dried Italian seasoning, salt, and freshly ground black pepper to create the marinade.

Cut and Toss: Cut the assorted vegetables into bite-sized pieces. Place them in a large bowl and drizzle the balsamic marinade over them. Toss the vegetables to ensure they are well coated.

Roast the Vegetables: Preheat your oven to 425°F (220°C). Spread the marinated vegetables evenly on a baking sheet lined with parchment paper. Roast them in the preheated oven for about 20-25 minutes or until they are tender and slightly caramelized, stirring once or twice during cooking.

Serve: Transfer the roasted balsamic vegetables to a serving platter, garnish with fresh basil leaves if desired, and serve hot. Enjoy the burst of flavors and textures!

Balsamic-Glazed Tofu

Balsamic-glazed tofu is a plant-based masterpiece that combines the meaty texture of tofu with the sweet and tangy allure of balsamic vinegar. This dish is perfect for those seeking a vegan protein source with a burst of flavor.

Ingredients:

- 1 block extra-firm tofu, pressed and cut into cubes
- 1/4 cup balsamic vinegar
- 2 tablespoons soy sauce (or tamari for a gluten-free option)
- 2 tablespoons maple syrup
- 2 cloves garlic, minced
- 1 tablespoon olive oil
- Salt and freshly ground black pepper to taste
- Fresh chives for garnish (optional)

Instructions:

Prepare the Glaze: In a bowl, whisk together the balsamic vinegar, soy sauce (or tamari), maple syrup, minced garlic, olive oil, salt, and freshly ground black pepper to create the glaze.

Marinate the Tofu: Place the cubed tofu in a shallow dish and pour the balsamic glaze over it. Ensure that the tofu is well coated. Cover the dish and refrigerate for at least 30 minutes to marinate.

Pan-Fry the Tofu: Heat a skillet over medium-high heat and add a bit of olive oil. Once hot, add the marinated tofu cubes and cook for about 3-4 minutes per side, or until they develop a golden crust and the glaze caramelizes.

Serve: Transfer the balsamic-glazed tofu to a serving platter, garnish with fresh chives if desired, and serve hot. Enjoy the mouthwatering flavors and the satisfying texture!

Stuffed Portobello Mushrooms with Balsamic Drizzle

Stuffed portobello mushrooms with a balsamic drizzle are a gourmet delight for vegans and vegetarians alike, featuring the earthy richness of mushrooms and the sweet tanginess of balsamic vinegar. This dish is perfect as an appetizer or main course.

Ingredients:

- 4 large portobello mushrooms, stems removed
- 1/2 cup breadcrumbs (use gluten-free breadcrumbs for a gluten-free option)
- 1/4 cup diced red bell pepper
- 1/4 cup diced red onion
- 1/4 cup chopped fresh spinach
- 2 cloves garlic, minced
- 1/4 cup balsamic vinegar
- 2 tablespoons extra-virgin olive oil
- Salt and freshly ground black pepper to taste
- Fresh basil leaves for garnish (optional)

Instructions:

Prepare the Mushroom Caps: Preheat your oven to 375°F (190°C). Place the portobello mushroom caps on a baking sheet lined with parchment paper. Brush them with a bit of olive oil and season with salt and freshly ground black pepper. Bake them in the preheated oven for about 15 minutes to soften slightly.

Prepare the Filling: In a skillet, heat the remaining olive oil over medium heat. Add the diced red bell pepper, diced red onion, and minced garlic. Sauté for about 2-3 minutes until the vegetables start to soften.

Combine and Stuff: In a bowl, combine the sautéed vegetables with the breadcrumbs and chopped fresh spinach. Season with salt and freshly ground black pepper. Mix well.

Stuff the Mushrooms: Remove the partially cooked portobello mushrooms from the oven. Fill each mushroom cap with the breadcrumb and vegetable mixture, pressing it down gently.

Bake Again: Return the stuffed mushrooms to the oven and bake for an additional 15-20 minutes, or until the mushrooms are tender and the filling is golden brown.

Drizzle with Balsamic: While the mushrooms are baking, heat the balsamic vinegar in a small saucepan over medium heat. Simmer for about 5-7 minutes until it reduces by half and becomes slightly syrupy.

Serve: Transfer the stuffed portobello mushrooms to a serving platter, drizzle with the balsamic reduction, and garnish with fresh basil leaves if desired. Serve hot and enjoy the gourmet flavors!

These vegetarian and vegan balsamic creations demonstrate the incredible versatility of balsamic vinegar in plant-based dishes. Whether you're following a plant-based diet or simply exploring new culinary horizons, these recipes will delight your palate.

Chapter 8: Balsamic in Soups and Stews

Enhance Your Comfort Food with Balsamic Vinegar

Balsamic vinegar brings a unique twist to classic soups and stews, elevating their flavors and adding a touch of sophistication. In this chapter, we'll delve into the world of warm and hearty dishes infused with the rich tanginess of balsamic vinegar.

Tomato Basil Soup with Balsamic Swirl

Tomato basil soup with a balsamic swirl is a comforting classic that gets a gourmet upgrade with the addition of a balsamic vinegar drizzle. This soup is a celebration of the harmonious pairing of tomatoes and balsamic vinegar.

Ingredients:

- 2 tablespoons olive oil
- 1 onion, diced
- 2 cloves garlic, minced
- 2 cans (28 ounces each) crushed tomatoes
- 4 cups vegetable broth
- 1/4 cup fresh basil leaves, chopped
- Salt and freshly ground black pepper to taste
- 2 tablespoons balsamic vinegar
- Fresh basil leaves for garnish

Instructions:

Sauté the Aromatics: In a large pot, heat the olive oil over medium heat. Add the diced onion and minced garlic. Sauté for about 2-3 minutes until the onion becomes translucent and fragrant.

Simmer the Soup: Add the crushed tomatoes, vegetable broth, and chopped basil leaves to the pot. Season with salt and freshly ground black pepper. Bring the mixture to a simmer and let it cook for about 15-20 minutes, allowing the flavors to meld.

Blend: Use an immersion blender or a regular blender to puree the soup until smooth and creamy.

Prepare the Balsamic Swirl: In a small saucepan, heat the balsamic vinegar over low heat until it becomes slightly syrupy, about 5-7 minutes.

Serve: Ladle the tomato basil soup into bowls. Drizzle the balsamic vinegar swirl over each serving and garnish with fresh basil leaves. Serve hot and enjoy the exquisite combination of flavors!

Balsamic-Infused Vegetable Stew

Balsamic-infused vegetable stew is a hearty and satisfying dish that highlights the natural sweetness of vegetables combined with the tangy richness of balsamic vinegar. This stew is a wonderful option for vegans and vegetarians.

Ingredients:

- 2 tablespoons olive oil
- 1 onion, diced
- 2 cloves garlic, minced
- 2 carrots, peeled and diced
- 2 potatoes, peeled and diced
- 2 cups diced tomatoes (canned or fresh)
- 4 cups vegetable broth
- 1/4 cup balsamic vinegar
- 1 cup green beans, trimmed and cut into bite-sized pieces
- 1 cup corn kernels (fresh or frozen)
- Salt and freshly ground black pepper to taste
- Fresh parsley for garnish (optional)

Instructions:

Sauté the Aromatics: In a large pot, heat the olive oil over medium heat. Add the diced onion and minced garlic. Sauté for about 2-3 minutes until the onion becomes translucent and fragrant.

Add the Vegetables: Add the diced carrots, potatoes, and diced tomatoes to the pot. Stir to combine with the aromatics.

Simmer the Stew: Pour in the vegetable broth and balsamic vinegar. Season with salt and freshly ground black pepper. Bring the mixture to a simmer, then cover and let it cook for about 20-25 minutes, or until the vegetables are tender.

Add the Green Beans and Corn: Stir in the green beans and corn kernels, and let the stew simmer for an additional 5-7 minutes until the green beans are crisp-tender.

Serve: Ladle the balsamic-infused vegetable stew into bowls, garnish with fresh parsley if desired, and serve hot. Enjoy the comforting and flavorful combination of vegetables and balsamic vinegar!

Balsamic Chicken Noodle Soup

Balsamic chicken noodle soup takes a classic comfort food to a whole new level with the addition of balsamic vinegar, creating a savory and tangy broth. This soup is perfect for chilly days or when you're feeling under the weather.

Ingredients:

- 1 pound boneless, skinless chicken thighs
- 8 cups chicken broth
- 2 carrots, peeled and sliced
- 2 celery stalks, sliced
- 1 onion, diced
- 2 cloves garlic, minced
- 1 cup wide egg noodles
- 2 tablespoons balsamic vinegar
- Salt and freshly ground black pepper to taste
- Fresh parsley for garnish (optional)

Instructions:

Poach the Chicken: In a large pot, combine the chicken thighs and chicken broth. Bring to a simmer over medium heat. Let the chicken simmer for about 15-20 minutes, or until it's cooked through. Remove the chicken from the broth, shred it with two forks, and set it aside.

Sauté the Aromatics: In the same pot, heat a bit of olive oil over medium heat. Add the diced onion, minced garlic, sliced carrots, and sliced celery. Sauté for about 2-3 minutes until the vegetables begin to soften.

Simmer the Soup: Pour the chicken broth back into the pot with the sautéed vegetables. Add the shredded chicken and egg noodles. Season with salt and freshly ground black pepper. Simmer for about 10-12 minutes, or until the noodles are cooked.

Finish with Balsamic Vinegar: Stir in the balsamic vinegar and let the soup simmer for an additional 2-3 minutes to incorporate the flavors.

Serve: Ladle the balsamic chicken noodle soup into bowls, garnish with fresh parsley if desired, and serve hot. Savor the heartwarming combination of chicken, noodles, and balsamic vinegar!

These soups and stews with a balsamic twist offer comfort and flavor in every spoonful. Whether you're in the mood for a classic tomato soup or a hearty vegetable stew, these recipes will warm your heart and soul.

Chapter 9: Balsamic Pasta Perfection

Elevate Your Pasta Game with the Magic of Balsamic Vinegar

Balsamic vinegar brings a delightful depth of flavor to pasta dishes, turning ordinary noodles into extraordinary culinary experiences. In this chapter, we'll explore three mouthwatering pasta recipes that showcase the versatility and richness of balsamic vinegar.

Balsamic Pasta Primavera

Balsamic pasta primavera is a vibrant and colorful dish that celebrates the beauty of seasonal vegetables combined with the sweet tanginess of balsamic vinegar. This recipe is a burst of flavors and textures on your plate.

Ingredients:

- 8 ounces pasta (your choice)
- 2 tablespoons olive oil
- 1 onion, diced
- 2 cloves garlic, minced
- 2 cups mixed vegetables (e.g., bell peppers, cherry tomatoes, zucchini, broccoli), chopped
- 2 tablespoons balsamic vinegar
- 1/4 cup grated Parmesan cheese (use a dairy-free alternative for a vegan version)
- Salt and freshly ground black pepper to taste
- Fresh basil leaves for garnish (optional)

Instructions:

Cook the Pasta: Cook the pasta according to the package instructions until al dente. Drain and set aside.

Sauté the Aromatics: In a large skillet, heat the olive oil over medium heat. Add the diced onion and minced garlic. Sauté for about 2-3 minutes until the onion becomes translucent and fragrant.

Add the Vegetables: Add the chopped mixed vegetables to the skillet. Sauté for 5-7 minutes, or until they become tender and slightly caramelized.

Combine with Balsamic Vinegar: Drizzle the balsamic vinegar over the sautéed vegetables and stir to coat them evenly. Cook for an additional 2 minutes to let the flavors meld.

Toss with Pasta: Add the cooked pasta to the skillet and toss to combine with the balsamic-coated vegetables.

Finish and Serve: Sprinkle the grated Parmesan cheese over the pasta, season with salt and freshly ground black pepper to taste, and toss again. Garnish with fresh basil leaves if desired. Serve hot and enjoy the explosion of colors and flavors!

Creamy Balsamic Fettuccine

Creamy balsamic fettuccine is a luscious pasta dish that marries the rich creaminess of Alfredo sauce with the sweet and tangy allure of balsamic vinegar. This recipe is comfort food at its finest.

Ingredients:

- 8 ounces fettuccine pasta
- 1/4 cup butter (or dairy-free alternative)
- 2 cloves garlic, minced
- 1 cup heavy cream (or coconut cream for a dairy-free version)
- 1/4 cup balsamic vinegar
- 1/2 cup grated Parmesan cheese (use a dairy-free alternative for a vegan version)
- Salt and freshly ground black pepper to taste
- Fresh parsley for garnish (optional)

Instructions:

Cook the Pasta: Cook the fettuccine pasta according to the package instructions until al dente. Drain and set aside.

Prepare the Sauce: In a large skillet, melt the butter over medium heat. Add the minced garlic and sauté for about 30 seconds until fragrant.

Add Cream and Balsamic: Pour in the heavy cream and balsamic vinegar. Stir to combine and let the mixture simmer for about 5 minutes, or until it thickens slightly.

Stir in Parmesan: Stir in the grated Parmesan cheese and continue to cook until the cheese is fully melted into the sauce. Season with salt and freshly ground black pepper to taste.

Toss with Pasta: Add the cooked fettuccine pasta to the skillet and toss to coat it with the creamy balsamic sauce.

Finish and Serve: Garnish with fresh parsley if desired. Serve hot and savor the creamy, balsamic-kissed pasta.

Balsamic and Sun-Dried Tomato Spaghetti

Balsamic and sun-dried tomato spaghetti is a flavorful and savory pasta dish that combines the intense flavors of sun-dried tomatoes with the tanginess of balsamic vinegar. This recipe is perfect for those seeking a bold and robust pasta experience.

Ingredients:

- 8 ounces spaghetti
- 2 tablespoons olive oil
- 1 onion, diced
- 2 cloves garlic, minced
- 1/2 cup sun-dried tomatoes (dry or oil-packed), chopped
- 2 tablespoons balsamic vinegar
- 1/4 cup fresh basil leaves, chopped
- Salt and freshly ground black pepper to taste
- Grated Parmesan cheese (use a dairy-free alternative for a vegan version)

Instructions:

Cook the Pasta: Cook the spaghetti according to the package instructions until al dente. Drain and set aside.

Sauté the Aromatics: In a large skillet, heat the olive oil over medium heat. Add the diced onion and minced garlic. Sauté for about 2-3 minutes until the onion becomes translucent and fragrant.

Add Sun-Dried Tomatoes: Add the chopped sun-dried tomatoes to the skillet. Sauté for an additional 2-3 minutes to soften and release their flavors.

Combine with Balsamic Vinegar: Drizzle the balsamic vinegar over the sautéed sun-dried tomatoes and stir to combine. Cook for an additional 2 minutes to let the flavors meld.

Toss with Spaghetti: Add the cooked spaghetti to the skillet and toss to coat it with the balsamic-infused sun-dried tomatoes.

Finish and Serve: Garnish with chopped fresh basil leaves and grated Parmesan cheese (or dairy-free alternative) if desired. Serve hot and enjoy the robust flavors of this pasta dish!

These balsamic pasta perfection recipes are a testament to the versatility and richness of balsamic vinegar in elevating pasta dishes to new heights of flavor.

Chapter 10: Balsamic Rice and Grains

Elevate Your Rice and Grain Dishes with the Tangy Touch of Balsamic Vinegar

Balsamic vinegar adds a burst of flavor and complexity to rice and grain-based dishes, turning them into culinary delights. In this chapter, we'll explore three delicious recipes that showcase the versatility and richness of balsamic vinegar in the world of grains.

Balsamic Risotto with Mushrooms

Balsamic risotto with mushrooms is a creamy and savory delight that combines the richness of risotto with the earthy flavors of mushrooms and the tangy touch of balsamic vinegar. This recipe is a celebration of comfort and sophistication.

Ingredients:

- 1 cup Arborio rice
- 1/4 cup butter
- 1 onion, finely chopped
- 2 cloves garlic, minced
- 8 ounces mushrooms, sliced
- 1/4 cup balsamic vinegar
- 4 cups chicken or vegetable broth, heated
- 1/2 cup grated Parmesan cheese (use a dairy-free alternative for a vegan version)
- Salt and freshly ground black pepper to taste
- Fresh parsley for garnish (optional)

Instructions:

Sauté the Aromatics: In a large skillet or saucepan, melt the butter over medium heat. Add the finely chopped onion and minced garlic. Sauté for about 2-3 minutes until the onion becomes translucent and fragrant.

Add Mushrooms: Add the sliced mushrooms to the skillet and cook for an additional 4-5 minutes until they become tender and browned.

Toast the Rice: Stir in the Arborio rice and cook for 1-2 minutes, allowing it to toast slightly.

Deglaze with Balsamic Vinegar: Pour the balsamic vinegar into the skillet, stirring constantly until most of it is absorbed by the rice.

Simmer with Broth: Begin adding the heated chicken or vegetable broth to the skillet, one ladleful at a time. Stir constantly and allow the liquid to be absorbed by the rice before adding more. Continue this process for about 20-25 minutes until the rice is creamy and cooked al dente.

Finish and Serve: Stir in the grated Parmesan cheese, season with salt and freshly ground black pepper to taste, and garnish with fresh parsley if desired. Serve hot and savor the creamy, balsamic-infused risotto.

Balsamic-Infused Quinoa Salad

Balsamic-infused quinoa salad is a refreshing and nutritious dish that combines the protein-packed goodness of quinoa with a medley of colorful vegetables and the tangy allure of balsamic vinegar. This salad is perfect for a light and satisfying meal.

Ingredients:

- 1 cup quinoa, rinsed
- 2 cups water
- 1/4 cup balsamic vinegar
- 2 tablespoons olive oil
- 1 red bell pepper, diced
- 1 cucumber, diced
- 1 cup cherry tomatoes, halved
- 1/4 cup red onion, finely chopped
- 1/4 cup fresh basil leaves, chopped
- Salt and freshly ground black pepper to taste
- Feta cheese crumbles (optional)
- Fresh basil leaves for garnish (optional)

Instructions:

Cook the Quinoa: In a medium saucepan, combine the quinoa and water. Bring to a boil, then reduce the heat to low, cover, and simmer for about 15 minutes, or until the quinoa is cooked and the water is absorbed. Remove from heat and let it cool.

Prepare the Dressing: In a small bowl, whisk together the balsamic vinegar and olive oil to create the dressing.

Combine Ingredients: In a large salad bowl, combine the cooked quinoa, diced red bell pepper, diced cucumber, cherry tomatoes, chopped red onion, and chopped fresh basil.

Toss with Dressing: Pour the balsamic dressing over the quinoa and vegetables. Toss to coat all the ingredients evenly.

Season and Garnish: Season the salad with salt and freshly ground black pepper to taste. If desired, garnish with feta cheese crumbles and fresh basil leaves.

Chill and Serve: Cover the salad and refrigerate for at least 30 minutes before serving, allowing the flavors to meld. Serve chilled and enjoy the vibrant, balsamic-infused quinoa salad.

Wild Rice with Balsamic Glaze

Wild rice with balsamic glaze is a hearty and flavorful dish that combines the nutty goodness of wild rice with a luscious balsamic glaze. This recipe is a celebration of natural ingredients and robust flavors.

Ingredients:

- 1 cup wild rice
- 3 cups water
- 1/4 cup balsamic vinegar
- 2 tablespoons honey (or maple syrup for a vegan version)
- 1/4 cup dried cranberries
- 1/4 cup chopped pecans
- Salt and freshly ground black pepper to taste
- Fresh thyme leaves for garnish (optional)

Instructions:

Cook the Wild Rice: In a medium saucepan, combine the wild rice and water. Bring to a boil, then reduce the heat to low, cover, and simmer for about 45-50 minutes, or until the rice is tender and most of the water is absorbed. Drain any excess water and set the cooked rice aside.

Prepare the Balsamic Glaze: In a small saucepan, combine the balsamic vinegar and honey (or maple syrup). Bring to a simmer over low heat and cook for about 5-7 minutes until the mixture thickens and becomes slightly syrupy.

Combine Ingredients: In a serving bowl, combine the cooked wild rice, dried cranberries, and chopped pecans.

Drizzle with Balsamic Glaze: Pour the balsamic glaze over the wild rice mixture and toss to coat everything evenly. Season with salt and freshly ground black pepper to taste.

Garnish and Serve: Garnish with fresh thyme leaves if desired. Serve warm and enjoy the delightful, balsamic-kissed wild rice.

These balsamic rice and grain recipes showcase the wonderful harmony of grains and balsamic vinegar.

Chapter 11: Balsamic Desserts

Sweet Surprises: Balsamic Vinegar in Desserts

Balsamic vinegar isn't just for savory dishes; it can also create delightful and unexpected flavor combinations in desserts. In this chapter, we'll explore three sweet recipes that feature the unique tanginess of balsamic vinegar.

Balsamic Berry Compote

Balsamic berry compote is a luscious and tangy topping that elevates your favorite desserts with the vibrant flavors of fresh berries and the sweet tanginess of balsamic vinegar. This compote is versatile and perfect for drizzling over ice cream, cheesecake, or pancakes.

Ingredients:

- 2 cups mixed berries (e.g., strawberries, blueberries, raspberries)
- 1/4 cup balsamic vinegar
- 2 tablespoons honey (or maple syrup for a vegan version)
- 1 teaspoon vanilla extract
- Zest of one lemon
- Fresh mint leaves for garnish (optional)

Instructions:

Prepare the Berries: Wash and hull the strawberries, if using. In a bowl, combine the mixed berries.

Create the Balsamic Glaze: In a small saucepan, combine the balsamic vinegar and honey (or maple syrup). Bring to a simmer over low heat and cook for about 5-7 minutes until the mixture thickens and becomes slightly syrupy.

Add Flavor: Remove the saucepan from heat and stir in the vanilla extract and lemon zest.

Combine with Berries: Pour the balsamic glaze over the mixed berries and gently toss to coat them evenly.

Chill and Serve: Cover the bowl and refrigerate the compote for at least 30 minutes to let the flavors meld. Serve the balsamic berry compote as a topping for your favorite desserts, garnished with fresh mint leaves if desired.

Balsamic Chocolate Truffles

Balsamic chocolate truffles are a decadent treat that combines the richness of dark chocolate with the tangy kick of balsamic vinegar, creating an exquisite balance of flavors. These truffles are perfect for special occasions or as a thoughtful gift.

Ingredients:

- 8 ounces dark chocolate (70% cocoa), finely chopped
- 1/2 cup heavy cream (or coconut cream for a dairy-free version)
- 2 tablespoons balsamic vinegar
- 2 tablespoons unsalted butter (or coconut oil for a dairy-free version)
- Cocoa powder or powdered sugar for rolling

Instructions:

Melt the Chocolate: Place the finely chopped dark chocolate in a heatproof bowl. In a small saucepan, heat the heavy cream (or coconut cream) over medium heat until it just begins to simmer. Pour the hot cream over the chopped chocolate and let it sit for a minute to melt the chocolate.

Create the Ganache: Stir the chocolate and cream mixture until it becomes smooth and glossy. Stir in the balsamic vinegar and unsalted butter (or coconut oil) until well combined.

Chill: Cover the bowl and refrigerate the ganache for at least 2-3 hours, or until it becomes firm enough to handle.

Form Truffles: Once the ganache has chilled, use a spoon or a melon baller to scoop out small portions. Roll each portion into a ball and place it on a parchment-lined tray.

Roll in Cocoa Powder or Powdered Sugar: Roll the truffles in cocoa powder or powdered sugar to coat them evenly. You can also drizzle a bit of extra balsamic vinegar on top for added flavor.

Chill and Serve: Refrigerate the truffles for another 30 minutes to firm them up. Serve chilled and savor the exquisite combination of dark chocolate and balsamic vinegar.

Balsamic Vanilla Ice Cream

Balsamic vanilla ice cream is a creamy and dreamy dessert that takes classic vanilla ice cream to the next level with the sweet and tangy notes of balsamic vinegar. This dessert is a perfect finale to any meal.

Ingredients:

- 2 cups vanilla ice cream (store-bought or homemade)
- 2 tablespoons balsamic vinegar
- Fresh berries or a drizzle of honey for garnish (optional)

Instructions:

Soften the Ice Cream: Allow the vanilla ice cream to soften slightly at room temperature for a few minutes, making it easier to work with.

Drizzle with Balsamic Vinegar: Drizzle the balsamic vinegar over the softened ice cream.

Swirl and Serve: Use a spoon or a spatula to gently swirl the balsamic vinegar into the ice cream, creating ribbons of flavor. You can also garnish with fresh berries or a drizzle of honey if desired.

Serve: Serve the balsamic vanilla ice cream immediately and enjoy the delightful contrast of creamy sweetness and tangy balsamic notes.

These balsamic desserts add an unexpected and delightful twist to your sweet indulgences. Whether you're looking for a fruity compote, luxurious truffles, or a simple ice cream upgrade, these recipes will satisfy your sweet tooth with flair.

Chapter 12: Cocktails and Mocktails with Balsamic Zing

Sip and Savor: Balsamic Vinegar in Beverages

Balsamic vinegar isn't limited to the kitchen; it can also create exciting and flavorful drinks. In this chapter, we'll explore three delightful cocktail and mocktail recipes that feature the tangy and fruity notes of balsamic vinegar.

Balsamic Berry Sangria

Balsamic berry sangria is a refreshing and vibrant cocktail that combines the sweetness of ripe berries with the tangy richness of balsamic vinegar and the fruity allure of red wine. This sangria is perfect for gatherings and warm summer evenings.

Ingredients:

- 1 bottle (750ml) red wine (e.g., Merlot or Cabernet Sauvignon)
- 1/4 cup balsamic vinegar
- 1/4 cup orange liqueur (e.g., Cointreau or Triple Sec)
- 2 tablespoons honey (adjust to taste)
- 1 cup mixed berries (e.g., strawberries, blueberries, raspberries)
- 1 orange, thinly sliced
- 1 lemon, thinly sliced
- 1 lime, thinly sliced
- 2 cups club soda or sparkling water
- Ice cubes
- Fresh mint leaves for garnish (optional)

Instructions:

Combine Ingredients: In a large pitcher, combine the red wine, balsamic vinegar, orange liqueur, and honey. Stir until the honey is fully dissolved.

Add Fruits: Add the mixed berries, thinly sliced orange, lemon, and lime to the pitcher. Stir to combine.

Chill: Cover the pitcher and refrigerate for at least 2-3 hours, allowing the flavors to meld.

Serve: Just before serving, add the club soda or sparkling water to the sangria. Fill glasses with ice cubes and pour the sangria over the ice. Garnish with fresh mint leaves if desired. Sip and savor the fruity and balsamic notes of this delightful drink.

Balsamic Mojito

Balsamic mojito is a zesty and herbaceous cocktail that combines the classic mojito flavors with the unique tanginess of balsamic vinegar. This mojito is a refreshing twist on a beloved cocktail.

Ingredients:

- 2 oz white rum
- 1/2 oz balsamic vinegar
- 1 oz fresh lime juice
- 2 teaspoons sugar (adjust to taste)
- 6-8 fresh mint leaves
- Soda water or sparkling water
- Ice cubes
- Lime slices and fresh mint sprigs for garnish

Instructions:

Muddle Mint and Lime: In a glass, muddle the fresh mint leaves and lime juice together to release their flavors. You can use a muddler or the back of a spoon.

Add Balsamic and Sugar: Add the balsamic vinegar and sugar to the glass. Stir to dissolve the sugar.

Build the Drink: Fill the glass with ice cubes. Pour in the white rum and top off the glass with soda water or sparkling water.

Stir and Garnish: Give the mojito a gentle stir to combine the ingredients. Garnish with a slice of lime and a fresh mint sprig.

Serve: Serve the balsamic mojito immediately and enjoy the zesty and tangy flavors of this unique cocktail.

Balsamic Fruit Spritzer

Balsamic fruit spritzer is a light and effervescent mocktail that combines the sweetness of fruit juice with the tangy depth of balsamic vinegar and the sparkle of club soda. This mocktail is perfect for those looking for a non-alcoholic and refreshing beverage.

Ingredients:

- 1/4 cup fruit juice (e.g., orange, cranberry, or pomegranate)
- 2 tablespoons balsamic vinegar
- 1 teaspoon honey (adjust to taste)
- 1 cup club soda or sparkling water
- Ice cubes
- Fresh fruit slices or berries for garnish (optional)
- Fresh mint leaves for garnish (optional)

Instructions:

Combine Ingredients: In a glass, combine the fruit juice, balsamic vinegar, and honey. Stir until the honey is fully dissolved.

Add Ice: Fill the glass with ice cubes.

Top with Club Soda: Pour in the club soda or sparkling water to top off the glass.

Stir and Garnish: Give the mocktail a gentle stir to combine the ingredients. Garnish with fresh fruit slices or berries and fresh mint leaves if desired.

Serve: Serve the balsamic fruit spritzer immediately and enjoy the fruity and tangy refreshment of this mocktail.

These balsamic-inspired cocktails and mocktails are a testament to the versatility of balsamic vinegar in creating unique and memorable beverages.

Chapter 13: Homemade Balsamic Marinades and Sauces

Elevate Your Dishes with Homemade Balsamic Creations

Homemade balsamic marinades and sauces have the power to transform your meals into culinary masterpieces. In this chapter, we'll explore three essential recipes that showcase the versatility and depth of flavor that balsamic vinegar can bring to your cooking.

Balsamic Glaze

Balsamic glaze is a versatile and syrupy reduction of balsamic vinegar that adds a rich and tangy sweetness to both savory and sweet dishes. This recipe is a kitchen essential that can elevate a wide range of recipes.

Ingredients:

- 1 cup balsamic vinegar
- 1/4 cup brown sugar (adjust to taste)
- Pinch of salt

Instructions:

Combine Ingredients: In a small saucepan, combine the balsamic vinegar, brown sugar, and a pinch of salt. Stir to combine.

Simmer: Place the saucepan over medium-high heat and bring the mixture to a boil. Reduce the heat to low and let it simmer for about 20-25 minutes, or until it reduces by half and becomes thick and syrupy.

Cool and Store: Remove the saucepan from heat and let the balsamic glaze cool to room temperature. It will continue to thicken as it cools. Transfer the glaze to a glass container with a tight-fitting lid and store it in the refrigerator.

Use: Drizzle balsamic glaze over salads, roasted vegetables, grilled meats, or even ice cream for a sweet and tangy enhancement to your dishes.

Balsamic BBQ Sauce

Balsamic BBQ sauce is a bold and tangy condiment that combines the smokiness of barbecue sauce with the complex flavors of balsamic vinegar. This sauce is perfect for grilling, dipping, or slathering on your favorite dishes.

Ingredients:

- 1 cup ketchup
- 1/2 cup balsamic vinegar
- 1/4 cup brown sugar
- 2 tablespoons Worcestershire sauce (or soy sauce for a vegetarian version)
- 2 cloves garlic, minced
- 1 teaspoon Dijon mustard
- 1/2 teaspoon smoked paprika
- 1/4 teaspoon cayenne pepper (adjust to taste)
- Salt and freshly ground black pepper to taste

Instructions:

Combine Ingredients: In a saucepan, combine the ketchup, balsamic vinegar, brown sugar, Worcestershire sauce (or soy sauce), minced garlic, Dijon mustard, smoked paprika, and cayenne pepper. Stir to combine.

Simmer: Place the saucepan over medium heat and bring the mixture to a simmer. Reduce the heat to low and let it simmer for about 15-20 minutes, or until the sauce thickens and the flavors meld.

Season: Season the BBQ sauce with salt and freshly ground black pepper to taste. Adjust the sweetness and spiciness by adding more brown sugar or cayenne pepper, if desired.

Cool and Store: Let the balsamic BBQ sauce cool to room temperature. Transfer it to an airtight container and store it in the refrigerator.

Use: Brush the balsamic BBQ sauce onto grilled meats, use it as a dip for chicken tenders or vegetables, or as a flavorful condiment for sandwiches and burgers.

Balsamic Marinade for Grilling

Balsamic marinade for grilling is a flavorful and versatile mixture that infuses your meats and vegetables with the sweet and tangy essence of balsamic vinegar. This marinade is perfect for enhancing the flavor of your grilled dishes.

Ingredients:

- 1/2 cup balsamic vinegar
- 1/4 cup olive oil
- 2 cloves garlic, minced
- 2 tablespoons honey (adjust to taste)
- 1 teaspoon dried thyme
- 1 teaspoon dried rosemary
- Salt and freshly ground black pepper to taste

Instructions:

Combine Ingredients: In a bowl, combine the balsamic vinegar, olive oil, minced garlic, honey, dried thyme, dried rosemary, salt, and freshly ground black pepper. Stir to combine.

Marinate: Place your choice of meats (e.g., chicken, beef, pork) or vegetables in a resealable plastic bag or a shallow dish. Pour the balsamic marinade over the ingredients.

Coat and Refrigerate: Ensure that the ingredients are coated evenly with the marinade. Seal the bag or cover the dish and refrigerate for at least 30 minutes, or ideally, for several hours to allow the flavors to penetrate.

Grill: Preheat your grill to the desired temperature. Grill the marinated meats or vegetables until cooked to your preferred level of doneness, basting with the remaining marinade as needed.

Serve: Plate your grilled dishes and serve hot, enjoying the balsamic-kissed flavors.

These homemade balsamic marinades and sauces are culinary essentials that can transform your dishes into gourmet creations.

Chapter 14: International Balsamic Influences

Exploring Balsamic Vinegar in Global Cuisines

Balsamic vinegar transcends borders and lends its unique flavor to dishes from around the world. In this chapter, we'll explore three international recipes that showcase the versatility of balsamic vinegar in different culinary traditions.

Balsamic Sushi Rolls

Balsamic sushi rolls offer a fusion of Japanese and Italian flavors, where the umami richness of sushi meets the sweet tanginess of balsamic vinegar. This unique twist on sushi will delight your taste buds.

Ingredients for Balsamic Glaze:

- 1/4 cup balsamic vinegar
- 2 tablespoons soy sauce
- 2 tablespoons honey
- 1 clove garlic, minced

Ingredients for Sushi Rolls:

- Sushi rice (prepared and seasoned)
- Nori (seaweed) sheets
- Assorted sushi fillings (e.g., avocado, cucumber, smoked salmon, crab sticks)
- Balsamic glaze (prepared)
- Sesame seeds (optional)
- Pickled ginger, soy sauce, and wasabi for serving

Instructions:

Prepare Balsamic Glaze: In a small saucepan, combine the balsamic vinegar, soy sauce, honey, and minced garlic. Bring to a simmer over low heat and cook for about 5-7 minutes until the mixture thickens and becomes slightly syrupy. Let it cool.

Assemble Sushi Rolls: Lay a bamboo sushi rolling mat on a clean surface. Place a sheet of plastic wrap on top of the mat. Lay a nori sheet, shiny side down, on the plastic wrap.

Spread Sushi Rice: Wet your fingers and spread a thin layer of sushi rice evenly over the nori sheet, leaving about half an inch of nori at the top edge.

Add Fillings: Arrange your choice of sushi fillings (e.g., avocado, cucumber, smoked salmon, crab sticks) in the center of the rice.

Drizzle with Balsamic Glaze: Drizzle a small amount of the prepared balsamic glaze over the fillings.

Roll Sushi: Using the bamboo mat, carefully roll the sushi, applying gentle pressure as you roll to ensure it holds its shape. Wet the exposed edge of nori to seal the roll.

Slice and Serve: Use a sharp knife to slice the sushi roll into bite-sized pieces. Optionally, sprinkle sesame seeds over the rolls for added texture.

Serve: Arrange the balsamic sushi rolls on a plate and serve with pickled ginger, soy sauce, and wasabi.

Balsamic Mediterranean Platter

A balsamic Mediterranean platter is a vibrant and flavorful combination of Mediterranean ingredients, elevated by the sweet tanginess of balsamic vinegar. This dish is a feast for the senses.

Ingredients:

- Hummus
- Falafel
- Cherry tomatoes, halved
- Cucumber, sliced
- Kalamata olives
- Feta cheese, crumbled
- Fresh basil leaves
- Balsamic glaze (prepared)

- Pita bread or flatbread

Instructions:

Assemble Platter: Arrange small bowls or plates with portions of hummus, falafel, cherry tomatoes, cucumber slices, Kalamata olives, crumbled feta cheese, and fresh basil leaves on a serving platter.

Drizzle with Balsamic Glaze: Drizzle the prepared balsamic glaze over the components of the platter to add a sweet and tangy touch.

Serve: Serve the balsamic Mediterranean platter with warm pita bread or flatbread for dipping and enjoying the rich Mediterranean flavors.

Balsamic-Infused Indian Curry

Balsamic-infused Indian curry brings the depth of balsamic vinegar to traditional Indian spices and ingredients, creating a harmonious fusion of flavors. This curry is a unique culinary experience.

Ingredients:

- 1 pound boneless chicken or tofu (cut into bite-sized pieces)
- 2 tablespoons vegetable oil
- 1 onion, finely chopped
- 2 cloves garlic, minced
- 1-inch piece of ginger, grated
- 1 teaspoon cumin seeds
- 1 teaspoon ground coriander
- 1/2 teaspoon ground cumin
- 1/2 teaspoon turmeric
- 1/2 teaspoon paprika
- 1/4 teaspoon cayenne pepper (adjust to taste)
- 1 cup tomato puree
- 1/4 cup balsamic vinegar
- 1/2 cup heavy cream (or coconut cream for a dairy-free version)
- Salt and freshly ground black pepper to taste
- Fresh cilantro leaves for garnish

- Cooked rice or naan bread for serving

Instructions:

Sear Chicken or Tofu: In a large skillet, heat the vegetable oil over medium-high heat. Sear the chicken or tofu pieces until they are browned on all sides. Remove them from the skillet and set aside.

Sauté Aromatics: In the same skillet, add the chopped onion and sauté for about 2-3 minutes until translucent. Add the minced garlic, grated ginger, and cumin seeds. Sauté for another 1-2 minutes until fragrant.

Add Spices: Add the ground coriander, ground cumin, turmeric, paprika, and cayenne pepper to the skillet. Stir to coat the onions and aromatics with the spices.

Tomato Puree: Pour in the tomato puree and stir to combine with the spice mixture. Cook for about 5-7 minutes, allowing the mixture to thicken.

Balsamic Vinegar: Add the balsamic vinegar to the skillet and stir to incorporate. Cook for another 2-3 minutes, allowing the balsamic vinegar to meld with the curry.

Cream and Simmer: Pour in the heavy cream (or coconut cream for a dairy-free version) and stir until the curry becomes creamy. Return the seared chicken or tofu to the skillet. Reduce the heat to low, cover, and simmer for about 15-20 minutes, or until the chicken is cooked through or the tofu is heated.

Season and Serve: Season the curry with salt and freshly ground black pepper to taste. Garnish with fresh cilantro leaves. Serve the balsamic-infused Indian curry with cooked rice or warm naan bread.

These international balsamic influences bring exciting new dimensions to traditional cuisines from Japan, the Mediterranean, and India.

Chapter 15: Preserving Balsamic Goodness

Unlocking the Power of Balsamic in Preservation

Preserving the rich flavors of balsamic vinegar allows you to enjoy its goodness in various ways throughout the year. In this chapter, we'll explore three preservation techniques that capture the essence of balsamic vinegar.

Making Balsamic Reductions

Balsamic reductions are concentrated, syrupy sauces that can enhance the flavor of a wide range of dishes, from salads to desserts. Making your own balsamic reduction is simple, and it allows you to have this versatile sauce readily available in your kitchen.

Ingredients:

- 1 cup balsamic vinegar
- 2 tablespoons honey (adjust to taste)
- Pinch of salt

Instructions:

Combine Ingredients: In a small saucepan, combine the balsamic vinegar, honey, and a pinch of salt. Stir to combine.

Simmer: Place the saucepan over medium-high heat and bring the mixture to a boil. Reduce the heat to low and let it simmer for about 20-25 minutes, or until it reduces by half and becomes thick and syrupy. Stir occasionally to prevent burning.

Cool and Store: Remove the saucepan from heat and let the balsamic reduction cool to room temperature. It will continue to thicken as it cools. Transfer the reduction to a glass container with a tight-fitting lid and store it in the refrigerator.

Use: Drizzle balsamic reduction over salads, grilled vegetables, roasted meats, strawberries, or even vanilla ice cream for a sweet and tangy burst of flavor.

Balsamic Pickled Vegetables

Balsamic pickled vegetables are a delightful way to preserve the crunch and flavor of seasonal vegetables while infusing them with the unique tanginess of balsamic vinegar. These pickled vegetables make for excellent snacks and additions to charcuterie boards.

Ingredients:

- Assorted vegetables (e.g., cucumbers, carrots, bell peppers)
- 1 cup balsamic vinegar
- 1/2 cup white vinegar
- 1/2 cup water
- 1/4 cup granulated sugar
- 2 cloves garlic, minced
- 1 tablespoon salt
- 1 teaspoon black peppercorns
- 1/2 teaspoon dried red pepper flakes (optional)
- Fresh herbs (e.g., dill, thyme, rosemary)
- Sterilized glass jars with lids

Instructions:

Prepare Vegetables: Wash and slice the assorted vegetables into thin rounds, sticks, or your preferred shape. Pack them tightly into sterilized glass jars, leaving some space at the top.

Create Pickling Liquid: In a saucepan, combine the balsamic vinegar, white vinegar, water, granulated sugar, minced garlic, salt, black peppercorns, and dried red pepper flakes if using. Bring the mixture to a boil over medium heat, stirring until the sugar and salt dissolve.

Pour Over Vegetables: Pour the hot pickling liquid over the prepared vegetables in the jars. Add a sprig or two of fresh herbs to each jar for added flavor.

Seal and Cool: Seal the jars with lids while the pickling liquid is still hot. Allow the jars to cool to room temperature.

Refrigerate and Wait: Refrigerate the balsamic pickled vegetables for at least 24 hours before enjoying them. They can be stored in the refrigerator for several weeks.

Serve: Serve the balsamic pickled vegetables as a snack, on sandwiches, or as a delightful accompaniment to charcuterie and cheese boards.

Balsamic-Infused Oils

Balsamic-infused oils are a simple yet flavorful way to capture the essence of balsamic vinegar for cooking and drizzling. These oils add depth to salad dressings, marinades, and roasted dishes.

Ingredients:

- 1 cup extra virgin olive oil (or another neutral oil)
- 1/4 cup balsamic vinegar
- A few sprigs of fresh herbs (e.g., rosemary, thyme, basil)
- 2 cloves garlic, peeled and smashed
- 1 dried red chili pepper (optional)
- Sterilized glass bottle with a tight-fitting lid

Instructions:

Combine Ingredients: In a saucepan, combine the extra virgin olive oil, balsamic vinegar, fresh herbs, smashed garlic cloves, and dried red chili pepper if using.

Heat Gently: Place the saucepan over low heat and warm the mixture gently. Allow it to steep for about 10-15 minutes, infusing the oil with the flavors of the herbs and balsamic vinegar. Do not let it simmer or boil.

Cool and Strain: Remove the saucepan from heat and let the oil mixture cool to room temperature. Strain the mixture through a fine-mesh sieve or cheesecloth into a sterilized glass bottle.

Seal and Store: Seal the bottle with a tight-fitting lid and store it in a cool, dark place. The balsamic-infused oil can be used immediately but will develop more flavor if allowed to sit for a few days.

Use: Drizzle balsamic-infused oil over salads, grilled vegetables, roasted meats, or use it as a flavorful dip for bread.

These preservation techniques allow you to enjoy the essence of balsamic vinegar throughout the year, whether through the rich syrup of balsamic reductions, the tangy crunch of pickled vegetables, or the flavor-enhancing balsamic-infused oils.

Chapter 16: Pairing Balsamic Vinegar with Food

The Art of Harmony: Discovering Perfect Balsamic Combinations

Pairing balsamic vinegar with various foods can unlock a world of flavor possibilities. In this chapter, we'll explore the art of pairing balsamic vinegar with cheese, meats, and desserts to create harmonious and delicious combinations.

Cheese and Balsamic Pairings

Pairing cheese with balsamic vinegar creates a symphony of flavors, as the tangy richness of balsamic vinegar complements the creamy, salty, and nutty notes of various cheeses. Here are some delightful pairings to savor:

Balsamic-Drizzled Parmesan: Drizzle aged balsamic vinegar over slices of Parmesan cheese. The sweet acidity of the balsamic enhances the umami and nuttiness of the cheese.

Fresh Mozzarella and Balsamic Reduction: Top slices of fresh mozzarella with a balsamic reduction and ripe tomato slices. The contrast of creamy cheese, sweet tomato, and tangy balsamic is a classic Caprese salad.

Goat Cheese and Balsamic Berries: Spread creamy goat cheese on crostini and top with balsamic-infused berries (e.g., strawberries, blueberries). The creamy-tart cheese pairs beautifully with the sweet-tangy fruit.

Gorgonzola and Balsamic-Soaked Figs: Serve crumbled Gorgonzola cheese alongside balsamic-soaked dried figs. The sharpness of the cheese balances the sweetness of the figs and balsamic.

Meats and Balsamic Combinations

Balsamic vinegar adds depth and complexity to various meat dishes, enhancing their flavors and creating a memorable culinary experience. Explore these meat and balsamic combinations:

Balsamic-Glazed Pork Tenderloin: Marinate pork tenderloin in a balsamic-based marinade before grilling or roasting. The sweet-tangy glaze creates a flavorful caramelized crust.

Steak with Balsamic Reduction: Drizzle a balsamic reduction over grilled or pan-seared steak. The richness of the meat is beautifully contrasted by the sweet and tangy reduction.

Chicken Caprese with Balsamic Drizzle: Prepare chicken breast or thighs with classic Caprese ingredients (tomato, mozzarella, basil), and drizzle with a balsamic glaze for a burst of flavor.

Balsamic-Glazed Salmon: Coat salmon fillets in a balsamic glaze before baking or grilling. The glaze caramelizes, creating a sweet and tangy crust on the salmon.

Dessert and Balsamic Duos

Balsamic vinegar can be a surprising and delightful addition to sweet treats, adding a layer of complexity and depth to desserts. Explore these dessert and balsamic duos:

Balsamic-Strawberry Shortcake: Layer fresh strawberries marinated in balsamic vinegar between slices of shortcake or angel food cake. The sweet-tangy berries complement the cake's sweetness.

Balsamic Chocolate Fondue: Add a splash of balsamic vinegar to your chocolate fondue for dipping fruits, marshmallows, and more. The acidity balances the richness of the chocolate.

Balsamic Berry Sorbet: Drizzle balsamic reduction over berry sorbet for an unexpected twist. The sweet-tangy contrast heightens the fruity flavors.

Balsamic Vanilla Ice Cream: Transform classic vanilla ice cream by adding a drizzle of balsamic reduction. The combination of creamy sweetness and tangy balsamic is a revelation.

These pairings showcase the versatility of balsamic vinegar in enhancing the flavors of cheese, meats, and desserts.

Chapter 17: Balsamic Vinegar Tasting Guide

Unlocking the Secrets of Balsamic Vinegar

Tasting balsamic vinegar is a sensory journey that allows you to appreciate its depth, complexity, and versatility. In this chapter, we'll guide you through the art of hosting a balsamic vinegar tasting, evaluating balsamic vinegar like a connoisseur, and discovering tasting notes with perfect pairings.

Hosting a Balsamic Vinegar Tasting

Hosting a balsamic vinegar tasting is a delightful way to explore the nuances of this versatile condiment and share the experience with friends and family. Here's how to create a memorable tasting event:

Select a Variety: Gather a selection of balsamic vinegars, including aged and traditional varieties. You can also include flavored balsamic vinegars for a diverse tasting experience.

Provide Accompaniments: Offer a selection of accompaniments such as fresh bread, cheeses, fruits (e.g., strawberries, figs), nuts (e.g., almonds, walnuts), and olive oil. These items will complement the tasting.

Set Up Tasting Stations: Arrange the balsamic vinegars and accompaniments at separate tasting stations. Label each vinegar with its name and age if applicable.

Tasting Sequence: Start with the youngest and lightest balsamic vinegar and progress to the older, more complex ones. This allows tasters to appreciate the evolving flavors.

Tasting Notes: Provide tasting cards for participants to jot down their observations, including appearance, aroma, flavor, and any pairing preferences.

Educate and Discuss: Offer information about the production process, aging, and tasting notes of each balsamic vinegar. Encourage discussion and sharing of impressions among participants.

Pair and Savor: Encourage guests to pair the balsamic vinegars with different accompaniments to explore how they complement or contrast with each other.

Share Impressions: After tasting, gather participants to share their favorite discoveries and pairings.

Evaluating Balsamic Vinegar

Evaluating balsamic vinegar requires attention to its appearance, aroma, flavor, and balance. Use this guide to assess the quality and characteristics of balsamic vinegar:

Appearance:

- Observe the color: Balsamic vinegar can range from pale amber to deep brown, depending on its age and production method.
- Note the consistency: It should be thick and syrupy, indicating quality and age.

Aroma:

- Inhale deeply: Take in the aroma and identify any notes of fruits, woods, or spices.
- Evaluate intensity: A well-aged balsamic vinegar will have a complex and pronounced fragrance.

Flavor:

- Taste a small amount: Let it coat your palate to fully experience the flavor.
- Note sweetness: Balsamic vinegar should have a balanced sweetness, not overpowering but with a pleasant sweetness that harmonizes with acidity.
- Recognize acidity: A good balsamic vinegar should have a

noticeable but not overwhelming acidity.

- Detect complexity: Evaluate the layers of flavors, including fruity, woody, and spicy notes.

Balance:

- Assess the harmony: A high-quality balsamic vinegar will have a well-balanced interplay of sweetness and acidity.
- Look for complexity: Aged balsamic vinegars should exhibit depth and complexity in their flavor profile.

Tasting Notes and Pairings

Each balsamic vinegar variety offers a unique flavor profile that can be enhanced through thoughtful pairings. Here are some tasting notes and pairing suggestions:

Young Balsamic Vinegar:

- Tasting Notes: Fresh, slightly tangy, and mildly sweet.
- Pairings: Use it in salad dressings, marinades for poultry and seafood, or drizzle it over fresh fruit.

Aged Balsamic Vinegar (5-10 years):

- Tasting Notes: Balanced sweetness with deeper, fruity flavors and a hint of oak.
- Pairings: Perfect for Caprese salads, drizzled over grilled vegetables, or as a dipping sauce for crusty bread.

Traditional Balsamic Vinegar (12+ years):

- Tasting Notes: Rich, complex, with a syrupy consistency. Notes of dark fruit, wood, and spices.
- Pairings: Enjoy it in its purest form, drizzled over strawberries, aged cheeses, or vanilla ice cream.

Flavored Balsamic Vinegar (e.g., fig, raspberry, citrus):

- Tasting Notes: A blend of balsamic complexity with the essence of the infused flavor.
- Pairings: Experiment with various dishes; for example, fig balsamic pairs well with grilled meats, while raspberry balsamic complements desserts.

White Balsamic Vinegar:

- Tasting Notes: Light, crisp, and slightly sweet with a mild acidity.
- Pairings: Ideal for light salads, seafood, and fruit-based dishes.

Hosting a balsamic vinegar tasting, evaluating the characteristics of balsamic vinegar, and discovering perfect pairings are enjoyable ways to deepen your appreciation for this versatile condiment.

Chapter 18: Balsamic Vinegar as a Gift

Sharing the Flavorful Gift of Balsamic

Balsamic vinegar, with its rich and complex flavors, makes for a delightful and thoughtful gift. In this chapter, we'll explore how to present balsamic vinegar as a gift, create beautiful balsamic gift sets, and craft homemade balsamic gift ideas that will delight your friends and loved ones.

Packaging and Presentation

The presentation of a balsamic vinegar gift is as important as the vinegar itself. Follow these tips for an attractive and appealing gift:

Choose Quality Bottles: Select clear glass bottles with secure caps or corks to showcase the rich color and texture of the balsamic vinegar. Ensure the bottles are clean and free from residue.

Personalize Labels: Create custom labels or tags that include the name of the balsamic vinegar, its age (if applicable), and a brief description of its flavor profile. Personalized labels add a thoughtful touch.

Wrap with Elegance: Wrap the bottle in a decorative wrapping paper, tissue paper, or a cloth napkin. Consider using natural materials like jute twine or raffia for a rustic touch.

Include Serving Suggestions: Add a small note or card with serving suggestions and pairings for the balsamic vinegar, helping the recipient explore its culinary possibilities.

Presentation Box: For a more formal gift, place the balsamic vinegar bottle in a sturdy presentation box or wooden crate. Line the box with tissue paper or straw for a rustic feel.

Seal with a Bow: Finish your gift with a ribbon or bow that matches the theme and occasion. A well-placed bow can elevate the overall presentation.

Creating Balsamic Gift Sets

Creating balsamic gift sets allows you to pair balsamic vinegar with complementary items, enhancing the overall gifting experience. Here are some ideas for balsamic gift sets:

Balsamic and Olive Oil Set: Pair a high-quality balsamic vinegar with an equally exquisite extra virgin olive oil. The combination is perfect for dipping bread, dressing salads, or enhancing various dishes.

Balsamic and Cheese Pairing: Include a bottle of balsamic vinegar alongside a selection of artisanal cheeses. Provide tasting notes and pairing suggestions to guide the recipient.

Balsamic and Gourmet Snacks: Combine balsamic vinegar with gourmet snacks like nuts, crackers, dried fruits, and chocolates. These sets make for delightful treats.

Balsamic and Cooking Accessories: Create a cooking-themed gift set by including balsamic vinegar with items like a wooden salad bowl, olive wood utensils, or a decorative salad dressing shaker.

Balsamic and Fresh Produce: Pair balsamic vinegar with a basket of fresh, seasonal fruits or vegetables. This set is perfect for those who love to experiment in the kitchen.

Homemade Balsamic Gift Ideas

Crafting homemade balsamic gift ideas allows you to add a personal touch and showcase your creativity. Here are some homemade gift ideas that feature balsamic vinegar:

Homemade Balsamic Glaze: Prepare a batch of homemade balsamic glaze and package it in small jars. Include recipe cards with ideas for using the glaze, such as drizzling it over grilled vegetables or ice cream.

Balsamic-Infused Oil: Create balsamic-infused olive oil by combining extra virgin olive oil with balsamic vinegar and herbs. Pour the oil into decorative bottles and seal with a cork or cap.

Balsamic Marinade Kit: Assemble a balsamic marinade kit with a bottle of balsamic vinegar, a jar of herbs and spices, and recipe cards for marinating various proteins and vegetables.

Balsamic-Infused Honey: Prepare balsamic-infused honey by combining honey and balsamic vinegar. Pour the mixture into small jars and label them. This sweet and tangy honey can be drizzled over desserts or used in marinades.

Balsamic-Infused Sea Salt: Make balsamic-infused sea salt by mixing sea salt with balsamic vinegar and allowing it to dry. Package the flavored salt in small jars or shakers.

Balsamic Vinegar Sampler: Create a sampler set by filling small bottles with different varieties of balsamic vinegar, such as aged, flavored, and white balsamic. Arrange them in a gift box with tasting notes.

Gift Wrapping and Presentation Tips

- Color Theme: Choose a color theme for your gift packaging and stick to it for a coordinated look.
- Natural Elements: Incorporate natural elements like twigs, pine cones, or dried flowers for a rustic or eco-friendly presentation.
- Cellophane or Tulle: Wrap your gift in transparent cellophane or tulle for a sophisticated touch, allowing the contents to show through.
- Handwritten Notes: Include a handwritten note or card expressing your well-wishes and the thought behind the gift.

Whether you're giving a single bottle of balsamic vinegar or crafting a custom gift set, presenting balsamic vinegar as a gift is a thoughtful way to share its flavors and versatility with others. Your creativity and attention to detail will make the gift even more special.

Chapter 19: Conclusion and Beyond

Savoring the World of Balsamic Vinegar

As our culinary journey through the world of balsamic vinegar comes to a close, it's time to reflect on the balsamic adventures we've embarked upon, consider further possibilities for your culinary exploration, and provide you with valuable resources and references to continue your balsamic voyage.

Recap of Balsamic Adventures

In this cookbook, we've delved into the world of balsamic vinegar, from its rich history and production methods to its diverse applications in the kitchen. Here's a recap of the balsamic adventures you've experienced:

Chapter 1: Balsamic Vinegar Basics laid the foundation by introducing the production process, aging, and proper storage of balsamic vinegar.

Chapter 2: Balsamic Vinegar in Salad Dressings elevated your salads with classic and creative dressing recipes.

Chapter 3: Appetizers with a Tangy Twist offered a tantalizing array of balsamic-infused appetizers.

Chapter 4: Balsamic-Glazed Meats showcased succulent meat dishes enhanced by balsamic glazes.

Chapter 5: Seafood Delights with Balsamic Flare explored the depths of flavor balsamic vinegar brings to seafood.

Chapter 6: Vegetarian and Vegan Balsamic Creations celebrated plant-based dishes elevated by balsamic magic.

Chapter 7: Balsamic in Soups and Stews demonstrated how balsamic can transform comforting soups and stews.

Chapter 8: Balsamic Pasta Perfection introduced pasta dishes that will forever change your pasta game.

Chapter 9: Balsamic Rice and Grains provided hearty and nutritious recipes featuring rice and grains.

Chapter 10: Balsamic Desserts unveiled the sweet side of balsamic, with luscious desserts.

Chapter 11: Cocktails and Mocktails with Balsamic Zing showcased refreshing beverages with a balsamic twist.

Chapter 12: Homemade Balsamic Marinades and Sauces empowered you with the skills to create your own marinades and sauces.

Chapter 13: International Balsamic Influences took your taste buds on a global tour of balsamic-infused dishes.

Chapter 14: Preserving Balsamic Goodness explored preservation techniques for balsamic vinegar.

Chapter 15: Pairing Balsamic Vinegar with Food revealed the art of harmonizing balsamic with cheese, meats, and desserts.

Chapter 16: Balsamic Vinegar Tasting Guide guided you in hosting tastings, evaluating balsamic, and discovering pairings.

Chapter 17: Balsamic Vinegar as a Gift provided insights into packaging, creating gift sets, and crafting homemade balsamic gifts.

Exploring Further Balsamic Possibilities

Your journey with balsamic vinegar doesn't have to end here. Continue your exploration by:

Aging Your Own: Consider aging your own balsamic vinegar at home using quality ingredients and traditional methods. It's a rewarding and creative process.

Visiting Balsamic Vinegar Producers: If you have the opportunity, visit balsamic vinegar producers in Italy or your local region. You can witness the traditional production methods firsthand.

Experimenting with Flavors: Try your hand at infusing balsamic vinegar with various flavors. Explore different fruits, herbs, and spices to create unique infusions.

Exploring Balsamic Varieties: Continue to discover different varieties of balsamic vinegar, including aged, flavored, and white balsamic. Each offers its own culinary possibilities.

Sharing Your Creations: Share your balsamic-inspired creations with friends and family. Encourage them to join you in your culinary adventures.

Resources and References

To further expand your knowledge and appreciation of balsamic vinegar, here are some resources and references:

Books: Explore books on balsamic vinegar, including historical accounts, culinary guides, and recipe collections.

Online Communities: Join online cooking and food communities where balsamic enthusiasts share their experiences and recipes.

Local Specialty Stores: Visit local specialty stores or farmers' markets that offer a variety of balsamic vinegars for tasting and purchase.

Cooking Classes: Enroll in cooking classes or workshops that focus on balsamic vinegar and its culinary applications.

Balsamic Vinegar Producers: Connect with reputable balsamic vinegar producers who can provide insights, guidance, and access to high-quality products.

As you continue your journey with balsamic vinegar, remember that culinary exploration is a never-ending adventure. The world of flavors and possibilities is vast, and balsamic vinegar is just one of the many treasures waiting to be discovered in your kitchen.

We hope this cookbook has inspired you to savor the rich flavors and versatility of balsamic vinegar in your culinary endeavors. Whether you're a seasoned chef or a home cook eager to experiment, balsamic vinegar invites you to create, innovate, and savor each delicious moment in your culinary journey.

Bon appétit and happy balsamic adventures!

www.ingramcontent.com/pod-product-compliance
Lightning Source LLC
Chambersburg PA
CBHW051247160726
47994CB00003B/1062